Maniac Magee

A guide for the novel by Jerry Spinelli
Great Works Author: Mary Ellen Taylor

SHELL EDUCATION

Publishing Credits

Corinne Burton, M.A.Ed., *President*; Emily R. Smith, M.A.Ed., *Editorial Director*; Lee Aucoin, *Multimedia Designer*; Stephanie Bernard, *Assistant Editor*; Don Tran, *Production Artist*; Amber Goff, *Editorial Assistant*

Image Credits

Dreamstime (cover)

Standards

© 2007 Teachers of English to Speakers of Other Languages, Inc. (TESOL)
© 2007 Board of Regents of the University of Wisconsin System. World-Class Instructional Design and Assessment (WIDA)
© Copyright 2010. National Governors Association Center for Best Practices and Council of Chief State School Officers.
All rights reserved.

Shell Education

5301 Oceanus Drive
Huntington Beach, CA 92649-1030
http://www.shelleducation.com
ISBN 978-1-4258-8983-8
© 2015 Shell Educational Publishing, Inc.
Printed in USA. WOR004

Table of Contents

How to Use This Literature Guide

Today's standards demand rigor and relevance in the reading of complex texts. The units in this series guide teachers in a rich and deep exploration of worthwhile works of literature for classroom study. The most rigorous instruction can also be interesting and engaging!

Many current strategies for effective literacy instruction have been incorporated into these instructional guides for literature. Throughout the units, text-dependent questions are used to determine comprehension of the book as well as student interpretation of the vocabulary words. The books chosen for the series are complex exemplars of carefully crafted works of literature. Close reading is used throughout the units to guide students toward revisiting the text and using textual evidence to respond to prompts orally and in writing. Students must analyze the story elements in multiple assignments for each section of the book. All of these strategies work together to rigorously guide students through their study of literature.

The next few pages will make clear how to use this guide for a purposeful and meaningful literature study. Each section of this guide is set up in the same way to make it easier for you to implement the instruction in your classroom.

Theme Thoughts

The great works of literature used throughout this series have important themes that have been relevant to people for many years. Many of the themes will be discussed during the various sections of this instructional guide. However, it would also benefit students to have independent time to think about the key themes of the novel.

Before students begin reading, have them complete *Pre-Reading Theme Thoughts* (page 13). This graphic organizer will allow students to think about the themes outside the context of the story. They'll have the opportunity to evaluate statements based on important themes and defend their opinions. Be sure to have students keep their papers for comparison to the *Post-Reading Theme Thoughts* (page 64). This graphic organizer is similar to the pre-reading activity. However, this time, students will be answering the questions from the point of view of one of the characters in the novel. They have to think about how the character would feel about each statement and defend their thoughts. To conclude the activity, have students compare what they thought about the themes before they read the novel to what the characters discovered during the story.

How to Use This Literature Guide *(cont.)*

Vocabulary

Each teacher overview page has definitions and sentences about how key vocabulary words are used in the section. These words should be introduced and discussed with students. There are two student vocabulary activity pages in each section. On the first page, students are asked to define the ten words chosen by the author of this unit. On the second page in most sections, each student will select at least eight words that he or she finds interesting or difficult. For each section, choose one of these pages for your students to complete. With either assignment, you may want to have students get into pairs to discuss the meanings of the words. Allow students to use reference guides to define the words. Monitor students to make sure the definitions they have found are accurate and relate to how the words are used in the text.

On some of the vocabulary student pages, students are asked to answer text-related questions about the vocabulary words. The following question stems will help you create your own vocabulary questions if you'd like to extend the discussion.

- How does this word describe _____'s character?
- In what ways does this word relate to the problem in this story?
- How does this word help you understand the setting?
- In what ways is this word related to the story's solution?
- Describe how this word supports the novel's theme of . . . .
- What visual images does this word bring to your mind?
- For what reasons might the author have chosen to use this particular word?

At times, more work with the words will help students understand their meanings. The following quick vocabulary activities are a good way to further study the words.

- Have students practice their vocabulary and writing skills by creating sentences and/or paragraphs in which multiple vocabulary words are used correctly and with evidence of understanding.
- Students can play vocabulary concentration. Students make a set of cards with the words and a separate set of cards with the definitions. Then, students lay the cards out on the table and play concentration. The goal of the game is to match vocabulary words with their definitions.
- Students can create word journal entries about the words. Students choose words they think are important and then describe why they think each word is important within the novel.

How to Use This Literature Guide (cont.)

Analyzing the Literature

After students have read each section, hold small-group or whole-class discussions. Questions are written at two levels of complexity to allow you to decide which questions best meet the needs of your students. The Level 1 questions are typically less abstract than the Level 2 questions. Level 1 is indicated by a square, while Level 2 is indicated by a triangle. These questions focus on the various story elements, such as character, setting, and plot. Student pages are provided if you want to assign these questions for individual student work before your group discussion. Be sure to add further questions as your students discuss what they've read. For each question, a few key points are provided for your reference as you discuss the novel with students.

Reader Response

In today's classrooms, there are often great readers who are below-average writers. So much time and energy is spent in classrooms getting students to read on grade level that little time is left to focus on writing skills. To help teachers include more writing in their daily literacy instruction, each section of this guide has a literature-based reader response prompt. Each of the three genres of writing is used in the reader responses within this guide: narrative, informative/explanatory, and opinion/argument. Students have a choice between two prompts for each reader response. One response requires students to make connections between the reading and their own lives. The other prompt requires students to determine text-to-text connections or connections within the text.

Close Reading the Literature

Within each section, students are asked to closely reread a short section of text. Since some versions of the novels have different page numbers, the selections are described by chapter and location, along with quotations to guide the readers. After each close reading, there are text-dependent questions to be answered by students.

Encourage students to read each question one at a time and then go back to the text and discover the answer. Work with students to ensure that they use the text to determine their answers rather than making unsupported inferences. Once students have answered the questions, discuss what they discovered. Suggested answers are provided in the answer key.

How to Use This Literature Guide *(cont.)*

Close Reading the Literature *(cont.)*

The generic, open-ended stems below can be used to write your own text-dependent questions if you would like to give students more practice.

- Give evidence from the text to support . . . .
- Justify your thinking using text evidence about . . . .
- Find evidence to support your conclusions about . . . .
- What text evidence helps the reader understand . . . ?
- Use the book to tell why _____ happens.
- Based on events in the story, ...
- Use text evidence to describe why . . . .

Making Connections

The activities in this section help students make cross-curricular connections to writing, mathematics, science, social studies, or the fine arts. Each of these types of activities requires higher-order thinking skills from students.

Creating with the Story Elements

It is important to spend time discussing the common story elements in literature. Understanding the characters, setting, and plot can increase students' comprehension and appreciation of the story. If teachers discuss these elements daily, students will more likely internalize the concepts and look for the elements in their independent reading. Another important reason for focusing on the story elements is that students will be better writers if they think about how the stories they read are constructed.

Students are given three options for working with the story elements. They are asked to create something related to the characters, setting, or plot of the novel. Students are given a choice in this activity so that they can decide to complete the activity that most appeals to them. Different multiple intelligences are used so that the activities are diverse and interesting to all students.

How to Use This Literature Guide (cont.)

Culminating Activity

This open-ended, cross-curricular activity requires higher-order thinking and allows for a creative product. Students will enjoy getting the chance to share what they have discovered through reading the novel. Be sure to allow them enough time to complete the activity at school or home.

Comprehension Assessment

The questions in this section are modeled after current standardized tests to help students analyze what they've read and prepare for tests they may see in their classrooms. The questions are dependent on the text and require critical-thinking skills to answer.

Response to Literature

The final post-reading activity is an essay based on the text that also requires further research by students. This is a great way to extend this book into other curricular areas. A suggested rubric is provided for teacher reference.

Correlation to the Standards

Shell Education is committed to producing educational materials that are research and standards based. As part of this effort, we have correlated all of our products to the academic standards of all 50 states, the District of Columbia, the Department of Defense Dependents Schools, and all Canadian provinces.

Purpose and Intent of Standards

Standards are designed to focus instruction and guide adoption of curricula. Standards are statements that describe the criteria necessary for students to meet specific academic goals. They define the knowledge, skills, and content students should acquire at each level. Standards are also used to develop standardized tests to evaluate students' academic progress. Teachers are required to demonstrate how their lessons meet standards. Standards are used in the development of all of our products, so educators can be assured they meet high academic standards.

How to Find Standards Correlations

To print a customized correlation report of this product for your state, visit our website at http://www.shelleducation.com and follow the online directions. If you require assistance in printing correlation reports, please contact our Customer Service Department at 1-877-777-3450.

Correlation to the Standards (cont.)

Standards Correlation Chart

The lessons in this guide were written to support today's college and career readiness standards. This chart indicates which sections of this guide address which standards.

College and Career Readiness Standards	Section
Read closely to determine what the text says explicitly and to make logical inferences from it; cite specific textual evidence when writing or speaking to support conclusions drawn from the text. (R.1)	Close Reading the Literature Sections 1–5; Creating with the Story Elements Sections 2, 4–5
Determine central ideas or themes of a text and analyze their development; summarize the key supporting details and ideas. (R.2)	Analyzing the Literature Sections 1–5; Creating with the Story Elements Section 2; Making Connections Sections 2, 4–5; Post-Reading Response to Literature
Analyze how and why individuals, events, or ideas develop and interact over the course of a text. (R.3)	Analyzing the Literature Sections 1–5; Post-Reading Theme Thoughts; Culminating Activity
Interpret words and phrases as they are used in a text, including determining technical, connotative, and figurative meanings, and analyze how specific word choices shape meaning or tone. (R.4)	Vocabulary Activity Sections 1–5; Close Reading the Literature Sections 2–3; Making Connections Sections 1, 3
Analyze the structure of texts, including how specific sentences, paragraphs, and larger portions of the text (e.g., a section, chapter, scene, or stanza) relate to each other and the whole. (R.5)	Making Connections Section 4; Creating with the Story Elements Sections 1–2
Write arguments to support claims in an analysis of substantive topics or texts using valid reasoning and relevant and sufficient evidence. (W.1)	Reader Response Sections 1–2, 4; Creating with the Story Elements Sections 3, 5; Culminating Activity; Post-Reading Response to Literature
Write informative/explanatory texts to examine and convey complex ideas and information clearly and accurately through the effective selection, organization, and analysis of content. (W.2)	Reader Response Sections 1–3, 5; Post-Reading Theme Thoughts
Write narratives to develop real or imagined experiences or events using effective technique, well-chosen details and well-structured event sequences. (W.3)	Making Connections Sections 1–2, 4; Reader Response Sections 3–5
Produce clear and coherent writing in which the development, organization, and style are appropriate to task, purpose, and audience. (W.4)	Post-Reading Theme Thoughts; Post-Reading Response to Literature

Correlation to the Standards (cont.)

Standards Correlation Chart (cont.)

College and Career Readiness Standards	Section
Draw evidence from literary or informational texts to support analysis, reflection, and research. (W.9)	Close Reading the Literature Sections 1–5
Prepare for and participate effectively in a range of conversations and collaborations with diverse partners, building on others' ideas and expressing their own clearly and persuasively. (SL.1)	Analyzing the Literature Sections 1–5; Making Connections Section 5
Determine or clarify the meaning of unknown and multiple-meaning words and phrases by using context clues, analyzing meaningful word parts, and consulting general and specialized reference materials, as appropriate. (L.4)	Vocabulary Sections 1–5
Acquire and use accurately a range of general academic and domain-specific words and phrases sufficient for reading, writing, speaking, and listening at the college and career readiness level; demonstrate independence in gathering vocabulary knowledge when encountering an unknown term important to comprehension or expression. (L.6)	Vocabulary Sections 1–5

TESOL and WIDA Standards

The lessons in this book promote English language development for English language learners. The following TESOL and WIDA English Language Development Standards are addressed through the activities in this book:

- Standard 1: English language learners communicate for social and instructional purposes within the school setting.

- Standard 2: English language learners communicate information, ideas and concepts necessary for academic success in the content area of language arts.

About the Author—Jerry Spinelli

If you were to ask a young Jerry Spinelli what he wanted to be when he grew up, his first answer would have been a cowboy. Later, he aspired to be a baseball player, but that all changed in eleventh grade. Instead of celebrating the high school football team's victory with his classmates, he wrote a poem about the event. After the poem "Goal to Go" was published in his hometown newspaper, Spinelli set his sights on a writing career.

Spinelli was born on February 1, 1942, in Norristown, Pennsylvania. He attended Gettysburg College in Pennsylvania where he was editor of the school literary magazine. After he acquired his master's degree in science from Johns Hopkins University, he wrote and edited for a department store magazine. In 1977, Spinelli married Eileen Mesi, who is also a children's writer.

For over twenty years, Spinelli worked at different jobs and wrote in his spare time— during lunch breaks, after dinner, and on weekends. His first four novels, intended for adults, were rejected, but his fifth novel, *Space Station Seventh Grade*, was published in 1988. It, too, was intended for adults, but a children's book publisher thought otherwise, and his career finally took off.

Spinelli has published more than 25 books. Two have garnered prestigious awards: *Maniac Magee* was awarded the 1990 Newbery Medal, while *Wringer* won a 1997 Newbery Honor. In addition, a movie version of *Maniac Magee* was produced and released on the Nickelodeon TV channel in 2003.

You can learn more about Spinelli by visiting his official website: **http://www.jerryspinelli.com**.

Possible Texts for Text Comparisons

Several other Spinelli novels also address the issues of being different and trying to fit in. Two of them are *Wringer* and *Stargirl*. In *Wringer*, we meet Palmer, a soon-to-be ten-year-old boy who despises the tradition that all ten-year-old boys must follow: They wring the necks of wounded pigeons during the town's annual pigeon shooting day. Palmer secretly keeps a pigeon as a pet and conceals it from his friends. Soon, he must make an important decision. *Stargirl* features a total nonconformist who, at first, intrigues an entire high school with her kind, sweet, and enchanting ways. She meditates, celebrates people's birthdays, and carries her pet rat to school. Everyone loves her—until they begin to turn on her.

Cross-Curricular Connection

This book lends itself well to the study of prejudice as well as to the issues of being different and trying to fit in.

Book Summary of *Maniac Magee*

Jeffrey Lionel Magee is only three years old when his parents die in a tragic accident while aboard the P & W high-speed trolley. His nearest relatives, Aunt Dot and Uncle Dan—an uptight, unhappy couple—take him in. For eight years, Jeffrey endures their strained relationship until he cannot take it any longer. During a spring musicale at his school, Jeffrey begins screaming when he sees Aunt Dot and Uncle Dan sitting on opposite sides of the auditorium. He runs out of the building, never to return.

After one year of running, Jeffrey finds himself in Two Mills, a town over 200 miles away from his former home. Two Mills is a town divided. The West End is where the white people live, while the black people live on the East End with Hector Street dividing the two. It is in the West End where Jeffrey earns a reputation as a "maniac" after he performs a series of amazing antics—from intercepting a football pass one-handed to rescuing a boy from Finsterwald's backyard. When he is chased into the East End, Maniac makes an enemy of Mars Bar Thompson but befriends Amanda Beale. It is Amanda's family who offers Maniac a place to stay. Everything is looking up for Maniac until Amanda's favorite book is destroyed and a racially motivated threat is written on the Beales' house. Fearing for the safety of his newfound family, Maniac runs away to the West End where he ends up sleeping at the zoo.

While living with the buffaloes at the zoo, an old park hand by the name of Grayson rescues Maniac. Their friendship blooms as Grayson teaches Maniac about baseball, and Maniac teaches Grayson how to read. Tragedy strikes when Grayson dies a few days after Christmas. Once again, Maniac is on the run.

His next encounter is with two young runaways, Russell and Piper McNab. Maniac finds himself living in their unkempt household and does his best to keep the two boys in school. Although the boys eventually banish Maniac from their house, they invite him to Piper's birthday party and tell him to bring a friend. Maniac goads Mars Bar Thompson to accompany him, and the results are disastrous as the Cobra gang members try to scare Mars Bar and call him names. Everyone is furious with Maniac, and he finds himself running once more.

Throughout the story, Maniac moves deftly between the two worlds, trying to show everyone that people are the same no matter their skin color. In the end, Maniac finds his permanent home with the Beale family.

Possible Texts for Text Sets

- Curtis, Christopher Paul. *Bud, Not Buddy*. Delacorte Press, 1999.
- Palacio, R.J. *Wonder*. Knopf, 2012.
- Stevenson, Sarah Jamila. *The Latte Rebellion*. Flux, 2011.
- Yang, Gene Luen. *American Born Chinese*. Square Fish, 2006.

Name _____

Date _____

Pre-Reading Theme Thoughts

Directions: Read each of the statements in the first column. Decide if you agree or disagree with the statements. Record your opinion by marking an X in Agree or Disagree for each statement. Explain your choices in the fourth column. There are no right or wrong answers.

Statement	Agree	Disagree	Explain Your Answer
Married couples should never divorce.			
If you witness someone being bullied, ignore the situation.			
Racial prejudice is a problem that exists only among adults in our society.			
Instead of facing a difficult situation head on, it is best to run from it.			

Vocabulary Overview

Ten key words from this section are provided below with definitions and sentences about how the words are used in the book. Choose one of the vocabulary activity sheets (pages 15 or 16) for students to complete as they read this section. Monitor students as they work to ensure the definitions they have found are accurate and relate to the text. Finally, discuss these important vocabulary words with students. If you think these words or other words in the section warrant more time devoted to them, there are suggestions in the introduction for other vocabulary activities (page 5).

Word	Definition	Sentence about Text
kaboodle (ch. 1)	a group, bunch, pack, or collection of things or people	Maniac's parents are killed in an accident when the entire **kaboodle** crashes into the river.
smatter (ch. 1)	a small amount	A **smatter** of giggling people greets Maniac when he screams during "Talk to the Animals."
grungy (ch. 3)	untidy	Amanda thinks that Maniac looks **grungy** with his torn shirt and broken shoes.
infamous (ch. 5)	well known for a bad quality	The Finsterwald home is **infamous** in the West End.
suffice (ch. 5)	to be enough	Sometimes it may not **suffice** to read directions only once.
blundering (ch. 5)	making a stupid mistake	Only a few unfortunate children find themselves **blundering** onto Finsterwald's property.
clamoring (ch. 5)	expressing noisily	Arnold Jones's body begins **clamoring** after he lands in Finsterwald's yard.
stupefied (ch. 5)	astonished; shocked	The high schoolers stand **stupefied** as Maniac rescues Arnold.
flinched (ch. 7)	made a quick movement in reaction to fear	McNab **flinches** when the baseball nips his cap.
maniac (ch. 8)	someone who behaves in a wild way	Jeffrey, the new kid in town, is nicknamed **Maniac**.

Name _____

Date _____

Understanding Vocabulary Words

Directions: The following words appear in this section of the book. Use context clues and reference materials to determine an accurate definition for each word.

Word	Definition
kaboodle (ch. 1)	
smatter (ch. 1)	
grungy (ch. 3)	
infamous (ch. 5)	
suffice (ch. 5)	
blundering (ch. 5)	
clamoring (ch. 5)	
stupefied (ch. 5)	
flinched (ch. 7)	
maniac (ch. 8)	

Name _____

Date _____

During-Reading Vocabulary Activity

Directions: As you read these chapters, record at least eight important words on the lines below. Try to find interesting, difficult, intriguing, special, or funny words. Your words can be long or short. They can be hard or easy to spell. After each word, use context clues in the text and reference materials to define the word.

- _____

- _____

- _____

- _____

- _____

- _____

- _____

- _____

- _____

- _____

Directions: Respond to these questions about the words in this section.

1. How are Jeffrey's actions suitable for his new nickname, **Maniac**?

   _____

   _____

2. What makes Finsterwald's backyard **infamous** in the West End?

   _____

   _____

   _____

Analyzing the Literature

Provided below are discussion questions you can use in small groups, with the whole class, or for written assignments. Each question is given at two levels so you can choose the right question for each group of students. Activity sheets with these questions are provided (pages 18–19) if you want students to write their responses. For each question, a few key discussion points are provided for your reference.

Story Element	■ Level 1	▲ Level 2	Key Discussion Points
Character	Characterize Jeffrey. Include his physical characteristics as well as abilities he displays.	Compare and contrast yourself to Jeffrey.	Jeffrey is described as a "scraggly little kid." He is often seen running with "the soles of both sneakers hanging by their hinges." He says hi to everyone he passes. He rescues Arnold Jones, carries a book everywhere, and intercepts Denehy's pass.
Plot	Tell what you have discovered about Jeffrey's home life.	Explain how Jeffrey's home life might have led him to run away.	After Jeffrey's parents die, he goes to live with his aunt and uncle who are not getting along well. They have two of everything, and they even split their time with Jeffrey. This makes Jeffrey upset and unhappy. He does not want to be split between the two, and likely longs for a cohesive family unit.
Setting	Describe Jeffrey's life on the run.	How do you think Jeffrey is able to survive on his own so far?	Jeffrey is spotted at the Little League field, at the deer shed in Elmwood Park Zoo, and even at the dinner table of a random family. Students may point out that Jeffrey is scrappy and resourceful.
Character	How does Jeffrey come to be called Maniac?	Maniac appears larger than life. What might be a more fitting name for Maniac? Defend your response.	Chapter 8 describes all the events leading up to Jeffrey's new name and describes people saying such things as, "Kid's gotta be a maniac." Some of these events may even feel exaggerated. Students may need to re-read this section to help them determine their responses.

Name _____

Date _____

◼ Analyzing the Literature

Directions: Think about the section you just read. Read each question and state your response with textual evidence.

1. Characterize Jeffrey. Include his physical characteristics as well as abilities he displays.

_____

_____

_____

_____

2. Tell what you have discovered about Jeffrey's home life.

_____

_____

_____

_____

3. Describe Jeffrey's life on the run.

_____

_____

_____

_____

4. How does Jeffrey come to be called Maniac?

_____

_____

_____

_____

▲ Analyzing the Literature

Directions: Think about the section you just read. Read each question and state your response with textual evidence.

1. Compare and contrast yourself to Jeffrey.

   _____

   _____

   _____

   _____

2. Explain how Jeffrey's home life might have led him to run away.

   _____

   _____

   _____

   _____

3. How do you think Jeffrey is able to survive on his own so far?

   _____

   _____

   _____

   _____

4. Maniac appears larger than life. What might be a more fitting name for Maniac? Defend your response.

   _____

   _____

   _____

   _____

Name _____

Date _____

Reader Response

Directions: Choose one of the following prompts about this section to answer. Be sure you include a topic sentence in your response, use textual evidence to support your opinion, and provide a strong conclusion that summarizes your opinion.

Writing Prompts

- **Opinion/Argument Piece**—Which do you believe is better: Living on the run like Maniac or living in one, specific home? Include examples to explain why your choice is better than the other.
- **Informative/Explanatory Piece**—What questions are you formulating about Maniac's life on the run? Write at least two questions and explain why you are curious about the answers.

_____

_____

_____

_____

_____

_____

_____

_____

_____

_____

_____

_____

_____

Name _____

Date _____

Close Reading the Literature

Directions: Closely reread chapter 3 from the beginning of the chapter through the sentence that begins, "First bell was ringing . . . ." Read each question below and then revisit the text to find evidence that supports your answer.

1. Cite text evidence to show that Jeffrey loves books.

   _____

   _____

   _____

2. Give examples based on text evidence to show why Amanda is suspicious of Jeffrey.

   _____

   _____

   _____

3. Use the text to tell why Amanda carries her books in a suitcase.

   _____

   _____

   _____

4. Explain why Maniac thinks Amanda is "different." Use examples from the text.

   _____

   _____

   _____

Name _____

Date _____

Making Connections–Writing a Legend

A legend is a very famous person. For example, Clark Gable is a screen legend for his role as Rhett Butler in the 1939 movie *Gone with the Wind*. A legend is also a story from the past that may or may not be true. In the book *Maniac Magee*, the main character is referred to as a legend. Furthermore, they say that the history of Maniac Magee is "one part fact, two parts legend, and three parts snowball."

Directions: Think of someone you know or have heard about that may fit the definition of a legend. Write your own narrative of events that show how he or she became a legend. Show how your character is part fact, part legend, and part snowball, just like Maniac. Be sure to include a snappy title or nickname for your character as well as a physical description of this person.

_____

_____

_____

_____

_____

_____

_____

_____

_____

_____

_____

_____

Name _____

Date _____

Creating with the Story Elements

Directions: Thinking about the story elements of character, setting, and plot in a novel is very important to understanding what is happening and why. Complete **one** of the following activities based on what you've read so far. Be creative and have fun!

Characters

Reread the section "Before the Story" that precedes the first chapter of the book. Note the use of hyperbole, or obvious exaggeration, in the first four sentences. Write a well-developed paragraph of your own that contains hyperbole to describe what you know of Jeffrey from the first nine chapters.

Setting

Aunt Dot and Uncle Dan hate each other, yet they will not divorce because they are strict Catholics. Soon, there are two of everything in the house, including two TVs, two refrigerators, and two toasters. Draw a map of what you think Aunt Dot's and Uncle Dan's kitchen looks like with dual appliances and utensils.

Plot

The plot of *Maniac Magee* follows a series of causes and effects. For example, when Jeffrey's parents die (the cause), he is forced to live with his Aunt Dot and Uncle Dan (the effect). Create a flow chart to show the series of causes and effects throughout the first nine chapters of the book. Begin with the deaths of Jeffrey's parents and end with him crossing Hector Street.

Vocabulary Overview

Ten key words from this section are provided below with definitions and sentences about how the words are used in the book. Choose one of the vocabulary activity sheets (pages 25 or 26) for students to complete as they read this section. Monitor students as they work to ensure the definitions they have found are accurate and relate to the text. Finally, discuss these important vocabulary words with students. If you think these words or other words in the section warrant more time devoted to them, there are suggestions in the introduction for other vocabulary activities (page 5).

Word	Definition	Sentence about Text
jutted (ch. 10)	protruded; stuck out, up, or forward	Mars Bar **juts** his chin towards a befuddled Maniac.
lingered (ch. 10)	delayed in quitting something	As the East End lady speaks to Maniac, a glare **lingers** in her eye.
scowling (ch. 11)	wrinkling the brow to show anger or disapproval	A row of **scowling** faces meets Maniac as he tries to protect Amanda's book.
finicky (ch. 11)	fussy; excessively elaborate	Maniac surmises that Amanda is quite **finicky** about her book.
quiver (ch. 12)	to move with a slight trembling motion	When Maniac realizes that Mr. Beale knows he is lying about his address, Maniac's lip begins to **quiver**.
solitude (ch. 14)	the state of being alone or remote from others	Maniac loves the **solitude** of his early morning runs.
converged (ch. 14)	came together from different directions to eventually meet	Everyone in the East End **converges** for the Fourth of July block party.
clotted (ch. 16)	thickened	The voice is sort of **clotted** as it calls Maniac a name.
slithered (ch. 18)	moved slowly with a twisting motion	An idea **slithers** into Amanda's brain; she will ask Maniac to stay.
contortions (ch. 19)	twists and bends	Cobble's Knot has more **contortions** than Albert Einstein's brain.

Name _____

Date _____

Understanding Vocabulary Words

Directions: The following words appear in this section of the book. Use context clues and reference materials to determine an accurate definition for each word.

Word	Definition
jutted (ch. 10)	
lingered (ch. 10)	
scowling (ch. 11)	
finicky (ch. 11)	
quiver (ch. 12)	
solitude (ch. 14)	
converged (ch. 14)	
clotted (ch. 16)	
slithered (ch. 18)	
contortions (ch. 19)	

Name _____

Date _____

During-Reading Vocabulary Activity

Directions: As you read these chapters, record at least eight important words on the lines below. Try to find interesting, difficult, intriguing, special, or funny words. Your words can be long or short. They can be hard or easy to spell. After each word, use context clues in the text and reference materials to define the word.

- _____
- _____
- _____
- _____
- _____
- _____
- _____
- _____
- _____
- _____

Directions: Respond to these questions about the words in this section.

1. Why are Mars Bar and his group **scowling** as they attempt to take Amanda's book from Maniac?

   _____

   _____

2. What events occur when the whole East End **converges** on the Fourth of July?

   _____

   _____

Analyzing the Literature

Provided below are discussion questions you can use in small groups, with the whole class, or for written assignments. Each question is given at two levels so you can choose the right question for each group of students. Activity sheets with these questions are provided (pages 28–29) if you want students to write their responses. For each question, a few key discussion points are provided for your reference.

Story Element	■ Level 1	▲ Level 2	Key Discussion Points
Plot	Describe what happens when Maniac runs into the East End to get away from McNab and his gang.	Mars Bar attempts to take Amanda's book from Maniac. What is Maniac's response? How is it unexpected?	When Mars Bar sees Maniac, he and his gang follow and confront Maniac and suggest that he should run away. Unafraid, Maniac stays. Most people faced with similar circumstances would probably run for safety.
Setting	List some things that Maniac loves about his new life with the Beale family.	Compare and contrast Maniac's life with Aunt Dot and Uncle Dan to his new life with the Beale family.	Mr. and Mrs. Beale pay attention to Maniac, unlike his own relatives. They buy him new sneakers and include him in family breakfasts, church going, and a block party. This contrasts with the joyless, separate existence led by Maniac's aunt and uncle.
Character	When Maniac moves in with the Beale family, he seems to blend right in. Describe some ways in which he makes himself at home.	Why do you think Maniac blends in so well in his new home with the Beale family?	Without being asked, Maniac quickly takes on household chores, cares for Hester and Lester, mows the grass, and keeps his room neat. Mrs. Beale is grateful for his help.
Character	In terms of race, describe how Maniac views himself.	Maniac seems oblivious to the fact that he is a white child living in a black neighborhood. How does this cause problems between himself and others?	In terms of race, Maniac views himself as not really white because of the different shades on his own skin. However, some people in the East End *are* aware of a race difference. They want Maniac to return to "his own kind" and they even call him names.

Name _____

Date _____

Analyzing the Literature

Directions: Think about the section you just read. Read each question and state your response with textual evidence.

1. Describe what happens when Maniac runs into the East End to get away from McNab and his gang.

   _____

   _____

   _____

   _____

2. List some things that Maniac loves about his new life with the Beale family.

   _____

   _____

   _____

   _____

3. When Maniac moves in with the Beale family, he seems to blend right in. Describe some ways in which he makes himself at home.

   _____

   _____

   _____

   _____

4. In terms of race, describe how Maniac views himself.

   _____

   _____

   _____

   _____

Name _____

Date _____

▲ Analyzing the Literature

Directions: Think about the section you just read. Read each question and state your response with textual evidence.

1. Mars Bar attempts to take Amanda's book from Maniac. What is Maniac's response? How is it unexpected?

_____

_____

_____

_____

2. Compare and contrast Maniac's life with Aunt Dot and Uncle Dan to his new life with the Beale family.

_____

_____

_____

3. Why do you think Maniac blends in so well in his new home with the Beale family?

_____

_____

_____

_____

4. Maniac seems oblivious to the fact that he is a white child living in a black neighborhood. How does this cause problems between himself and others?

_____

_____

_____

Name _____

Date _____

Reader Response

Directions: Choose one of the following prompts about this section to answer. Be sure you include a topic sentence in your response, use textual evidence to support your opinion, and provide a strong conclusion that summarizes your opinion.

Writing Prompts

- **Opinion/Argument Piece**—Of all the things Maniac loves about his new life with the Beale family, which would be most important to you? Include examples to support your choice.
- **Informative/Explanatory Piece**—Maniac is blind. "He could see things, but he couldn't see what they meant." Explain how this philosophy might cause problems for Maniac in the future.

_____

_____

_____

_____

_____

_____

_____

_____

_____

_____

_____

_____

_____

_____

_____

Name _____

Date _____

Close Reading the Literature

Directions: Closely reread chapter 14 beginning with the line, "He loved the noise of the church they went to on Sunday mornings . . . ." Stop at the end of the chapter. Read each question and then revisit the text to find evidence that supports your answer.

1. Give evidence from the text to demonstrate how Maniac loves his new life.

   _____

   _____

   _____

2. How do you know that Maniac does not want to lose his name? Support your answer with reference to the text.

   _____

   _____

   _____

3. What evidence can you find to show how Maniac is living up to his nickname?

   _____

   _____

   _____

4. Cite text evidence that helps the reader understand how church makes Maniac feel.

   _____

   _____

   _____

Name _____

Date _____

Making Connections—Writing a Characterization

Directions: Maniac is a complex character. For example, not only is he helpful around the Beale household, but he also possesses some unusual traits and skills, such as the ability to untie complicated knots. Fill in the spaces of the chart below with text evidence from chapters 10–21 to show how Maniac exhibits each trait listed.

Trait	Maniac's Words and/or Actions
respectful	
helpful	
skillful	
famous	
likeable	
"color" blind	
protective	
resourceful	

Creating with the Story Elements

Directions: Thinking about the story elements of character, setting, and plot in a novel is very important to understanding what is happening and why. Complete **one** of the following activities based on what you've read so far. Be creative and have fun!

Characters

Amanda is upset when Maniac tries to leave. She provides him with several reasons why he should not go, but he answers with indifference. Pretend you are Amanda. Write Maniac a heartfelt letter outlining several benefits for him to stay with the Beale family.

Setting

The Beale household works just fine before Maniac arrives, but things change once he moves in. For example, before Maniac's arrival, Mrs. Beale spends a lot of time cleaning up after Hester and Lester's crayon markings. But after Maniac's arrival, the children lose interest in coloring. Make a before-and-after chart showing even more changes Maniac brings to the household.

Plot

Identify and summarize the major events that cause Maniac to leave his comfy home with the Beale family. Draw a cartoon strip to show the progression of these events.

Vocabulary Overview

Ten key words from this section are provided below with definitions and sentences about how the words are used in the book. Choose one of the vocabulary activity sheets (pages 35 or 36) for students to complete as they read this section. Monitor students as they work to ensure the definitions they have found are accurate and relate to the text. Finally, discuss these important vocabulary words with students. If you think these words or other words in the section warrant more time devoted to them, there are suggestions in the introduction for other vocabulary activities (page 5).

Word	Definition	Sentence about Text
prompt (ch. 23)	act without delay	When Grayson asks Maniac where he is going to live, Maniac gives a **prompt** answer.
dumbfounded (ch. 24)	astonished; surprised	Grayson is **dumbfounded** when Maniac says that he is ready to eat again.
abruptly (ch. 24)	suddenly and unexpectedly	While Maniac eats dessert, Grayson **abruptly** asks him about the Beale family.
sleazy (ch. 25)	dirty and seedy	Grayson relates stories about the **sleazy** accommodations he encountered during his early baseball career.
immortality (ch. 25)	being famous for a long time	After Grayson strikes out Willie Mays in his last at-bat in the minors, Grayson achieves baseball **immortality**.
repertoire (ch. 26)	series or range of works performed regularly	Grayson's pitching **repertoire** includes the "stopball."
preposterous (ch. 28)	outrageous; completely ridiculous	Staying overnight in the band shell seems like a **preposterous** idea to Grayson.
languished (ch. 30)	weakened; declined	Because their tree-trimming instincts had **languished** for so long, Grayson and Maniac over-decorate the tree.
meandering (ch. 31)	wandering aimlessly	On Christmas morning, Grayson and Maniac find themselves **meandering** through the park and to the zoo.
stoic (ch. 32)	being able to endure hardship without showing any feelings	Despite the downturn of events in his life, Grayson remains **stoic**.

Name _____

Date _____

Understanding Vocabulary Words

Directions: The following words appear in this section of the book. Use context clues and reference materials to determine an accurate definition for each word.

Word	Definition
prompt (ch. 23)	
dumbfounded (ch. 24)	
abruptly (ch. 24)	
sleazy (ch. 25)	
immortality (ch. 25)	
repertoire (ch. 26)	
preposterous (ch. 28)	
languished (ch. 30)	
meandering (ch. 31)	
stoic (ch. 32)	

Name _____

Date _____

During-Reading Vocabulary Activity

Directions: As you read these chapters, record at least eight important words on the lines below. Try to find interesting, difficult, intriguing, special, or funny words. Your words can be long or short. They can be hard or easy to spell. After each word, use context clues in the text and reference materials to define the word.

- _____

- _____

- _____

- _____

- _____

- _____

- _____

- _____

- _____

- _____

Directions: Now, organize your words. Rewrite each of your words on a sticky note. Work as a group to create a bar graph of your words. You should stack any words that are the same on top of one another. Different words appear in different columns. Finally, discuss with a group why certain words were chosen more often than other words.

Analyzing the Literature

Provided below are discussion questions you can use in small groups, with the whole class, or for written assignments. Each question is given at two levels so you can choose the right question for each group of students. Activity sheets with these questions are provided (pages 38–39) if you want students to write their responses. For each question, a few key discussion points are provided for your reference.

Story Element	■ Level 1	▲ Level 2	Key Discussion Points
Setting	Discuss what happens after Grayson finds Maniac lying in front of the buffalo pen at the zoo.	Think about Maniac's home in the baseball room when he first stays there. How does it change over time to become a "real" home?	Grayson takes Maniac back to his home at the YMCA where Maniac showers for a long time. Since Grayson cannot let Maniac stay with him, he sets him up in the baseball room. Gradually, Grayson brings in appliances and furniture, and later he moves in himself.
Characters	Describe the early relationship between Maniac and Grayson. Describe changes in the relationship by the end of chapter 30.	In what ways does the relationship change between Maniac and Grayson? Include a discussion of the turning point where they reverse roles.	From the time he finds Maniac at the zoo, Grayson takes care of Maniac. He feeds him, clothes him, buys him home furnishings, and teaches him to pitch a "stopball." When Grayson asks Maniac to teach him to read, their roles reverse, as Maniac now becomes the teacher and nurturer.
Characters	Who is Grayson? How would you describe him?	At first, Grayson will not tell Maniac any details of his life. Why do you think he is so reluctant to reveal anything about his past?	Grayson is an old park hand who once had a promising baseball career, but a series of unusually unlucky events prevents that from happening. Through it all, Grayson remains stoic and does not reveal much of himself to others because he is ashamed and feels he has disgraced himself.
Plot	How does Maniac feel about the baseball glove that Grayson gives him as a Christmas present?	Describe the significance of Grayson's gift of his old baseball glove.	Maniac is overjoyed and it is not just because he likes baseball. He realizes that this is a piece of history; the glove that Grayson had played with in the minors. Because it has so much meaning for Grayson, it also means a lot to Maniac.

Name _____

Date _____

Analyzing the Literature

Directions: Think about the section you just read. Read each question and state your response with textual evidence.

1. Discuss what happens after Grayson finds Maniac lying in front of the buffalo pen at the zoo.

_____

_____

_____

2. Describe the early relationship between Maniac and Grayson. Describe any changes in the relationship by the end of chapter 30.

_____

_____

_____

3. Who is Grayson? How would you describe him?

_____

_____

_____

4. How does Maniac feel about the baseball glove that Grayson gives him as a Christmas present?

_____

_____

_____

Name _____

Date _____

▲ Analyzing the Literature

Directions: Think about the section you just read. Read each question and state your response with textual evidence.

1. Think about Maniac's home in the baseball room when he first stays there. How does it change over time to become a "real" home?

   _____

   _____

   _____

2. In what ways does the relationship change between Maniac and Grayson? Include a discussion of the turning point where they reverse roles.

   _____

   _____

   _____

3. At first, Grayson will not tell Maniac any details of his life. Why do you think he is so reluctant to reveal anything about his past?

   _____

   _____

   _____

   _____

4. Describe the significance of Grayson's gift of his old baseball glove.

   _____

   _____

   _____

   _____

Name _____

Date _____

Reader Response

Directions: Choose one of the following prompts about this section to answer. Be sure you include a topic sentence in your response, use textual evidence to support your opinion, and provide a strong conclusion that summarizes your opinion.

Writing Prompts

- **Narrative Piece**—Maniac tells Grayson the story of his life. What is your life story? In what ways is your story similar to or different from Maniac's?
- **Informative/Explanatory Piece**—Maniac is surprised to learn that Grayson cannot read. Explain how Grayson's illiteracy contributes to the problems in his life and his ability to provide for himself.

_____

_____

_____

_____

_____

_____

_____

_____

_____

_____

_____

_____

_____

_____

_____

Close Reading the Literature

Directions: Closely reread chapter 23. Read each question and then revisit the text to find evidence that supports your answer.

1. Cite the text to show how Maniac reacts when Grayson brings up the subject of school.

   _____

   _____

   _____

2. Use the text to support the characterization of Grayson as kind and generous.

   _____

   _____

   _____

3. Based on evidence you find in the text, describe what school means to Maniac.

   _____

   _____

   _____

4. What text evidence helps the reader understand that Grayson thinks that Maniac is a lot like him?

   _____

   _____

   _____

Name _____

Date _____

Making Connections–Writing a Newspaper Article

Willie Mays was a famous African American baseball player during the 1950s through the 1970s. After he retired, he was inducted into the National Baseball Hall of Fame. In *Maniac Magee*, Mays plays a pivotal role in Grayson's life when Grayson strikes out Mays at his last at-bat in the minor leagues. Chapter 25 of *Maniac Magee* focuses on this event and some of the other baseball stories that Grayson shares with Maniac.

Directions: Reread chapter 25. On a separate sheet of paper, make a list of all the baseball-related words you can find, and write a definition for each one. Consult a dictionary or a baseball handbook, if necessary. Continue your research to find out more about baseball star Willie Mays. Research and gather evidence for each of the five questions below. Finally, on another sheet of paper, write a newspaper article that incorporates the 5 Ws you have researched as well as the baseball words you defined.

Question	Notes for Willie Mays Article
Who was his family?	
What awards did he win?	
What records does he hold?	
Where did he play?	
When did he live?	
Why is he still remembered today?	

Creating with the Story Elements

Directions: Thinking about the story elements of character, setting, and plot in a novel is very important to understanding what is happening and why. Complete **one** of the following activities based on what you've read so far. Be creative and have fun!

Characters

When Grayson asks Maniac to teach him to read, Maniac uses picture books to help him learn. For Christmas, Maniac writes a book, *The Man Who Struck Out Willie Mays*, for Grayson. Create your own picture book about a special event in your life. Be sure to illustrate and color your pictures of this event.

Setting

At first, the baseball room is rather bare, and Maniac uses chest protectors for a mattress. Gradually, Grayson furnishes the area with a chest of drawers, a space heater, a toaster oven, a small refrigerator, blankets, paper plates and plastic utensils, and a mat to sleep on. Draw a picture of how you imagine the interior of 101 Band Shell Boulevard looks.

Plot

Grayson wants Maniac to attend school, but Maniac stubbornly refuses. Do research to find facts and statistics that support the advantages of staying in school. Use the evidence you gather to write a speech you would give to Maniac to convince him to go to school.

Vocabulary Overview

Ten key words from this section are provided below with definitions and sentences about how the words are used in the book. Choose one of the vocabulary activity sheets (pages 45 or 46) for students to complete as they read this section. Monitor students as they work to ensure the definitions they have found are accurate and relate to the text. Finally, discuss these important vocabulary words with students. If you think these words or other words in the section warrant more time devoted to them, there are suggestions in the introduction for other vocabulary activities (page 5).

Word	Definition	Sentence about Text
nonperishable (ch. 33)	unlikely to rot or decay	Maniac returns to the band shell only long enough to pick up some **nonperishable** food.
replicas (ch. 33)	exact copies of something, such as a statue	At Valley Forge, Maniac sees **replicas** of the Continental Army's shelters.
embedded (ch. 34)	fixed firmly in the surrounding area	Screecher's voice is loud and sounds as if a microphone is **embedded** in his throat.
lambasting (ch. 35)	criticizing harshly	John McNab finishes **lambasting** his two brothers for running away.
nonchalantly (ch. 35)	calm and relaxed	When John's father yells angrily, John responds **nonchalantly**.
prone (ch. 35)	lying flat and facing downwards	Russell and Piper lie **prone** as they fire toy submachine guns.
portal (ch. 36)	a large, impressive doorway	Maniac climbs the three cement steps to the white door, the **portal** of death.
perilous (ch. 37)	dangerous; risky	The McNabs issue Maniac the most **perilous** challenge of all—to go into the East End.
forlorn (ch. 38)	sad and lonely	After the rain, the **forlorn** worms are marooned on the concrete and asphalt.
pandemonium (ch. 38)	uproar and confusion	Mars Bar's protests are drowned in the **pandemonium** following the race.

Name _____

Date _____

Understanding Vocabulary Words

Directions: The following words appear in this section of the book. Use context clues and reference materials to determine an accurate definition for each word.

Word	Definition
nonperishable (ch. 33)	
replicas (ch. 33)	
embedded (ch. 34)	
lambasting (ch. 35)	
nonchalantly (ch. 35)	
prone (ch. 35)	
portal (ch. 36)	
perilous (ch. 37)	
forlorn (ch. 38)	
pandemonium (ch. 38)	

Name _____

Date _____

During-Reading Vocabulary Activity

Directions: As you read these chapters, record at least eight important words on the lines below. Try to find interesting, difficult, intriguing, special, or funny words. Your words can be long or short. They can be hard or easy to spell. After each word, use context clues in the text and reference materials to define the word.

- _____

- _____

- _____

- _____

- _____

- _____

- _____

- _____

- _____

- _____

Directions: Respond to these questions about the words in this section.

1. In what way is Russell and Piper's challenge for Maniac to enter the East End the most **perilous** challenge of all?

   _____

   _____

2. Describe the **pandemonium** following the race between Mars Bar and Maniac.

   _____

   _____

Analyzing the Literature

Provided below are discussion questions you can use in small groups, with the whole class, or for written assignments. Each question is given at two levels so you can choose the right question for each group of students. Activity sheets with these questions are provided (pages 48–49) if you want students to write their responses. For each question, a few key discussion points are provided for your reference.

Story Element	■ Level 1	▲ Level 2	Key Discussion Points
Plot	What is it like for Maniac to be on the run after Grayson dies?	How is Maniac's journey different now from when he initially goes on the run at the beginning of the book?	Maniac drifts and wanders in all directions, sleeping in a variety of places including the buffalo pen at the zoo and a basement stairwell. He feeds himself at the zoo and the Salvation Army and does odd jobs. Although his journey takes Maniac to some of his old haunts, he is no longer looking for a home and is now waiting for death.
Character	Describe Russell and Piper.	In what ways are Russell and Piper like Maniac?	The boys are loud, exuberant brothers who like to fight physically, bicker, and say mean things to others. Like Maniac, they are not in school, they are runaways, and they carry a sack of essentials, which contains mostly food treats.
Setting	What story details help you picture what it is like inside the McNab household?	How does Maniac feel about the living conditions at the McNab's?	Discuss the presence of cockroaches and animal urine and feces covering the bare floor. Cans, bottles, peelings, and wrappers lie everywhere. There is a hole in the ceiling and peeling paint comes off like cornflakes. Maniac remembers his happier times with Hester and Lester, and with Grayson. The first night, he fearfully falls asleep.
Character	How does Mars Bar react when he first sees Maniac?	Maniac regrets embarrassing Mars Bar in the race. Why?	Mars Bar tells Maniac how "bad" he is and asks Maniac to race him. Maniac wins, thus embarrassing Mars Bar. Maniac regrets disgracing his opponent because he does not feel right paying back Mars Bar for his nastiness. Also, Maniac is unsure how the crowd will react to his win.

Name _____

Date _____

Analyzing the Literature

Directions: Think about the section you just read. Read each question and state your response with textual evidence.

1. What is it like for Maniac to be on the run after Grayson dies?

_____

_____

_____

_____

2. Describe Russell and Piper.

_____

_____

_____

_____

3. What story details help you picture what it is like inside the McNab household?

_____

_____

_____

_____

4. How does Mars Bar react when he first sees Maniac?

_____

_____

_____

_____

Name _____

Date _____

▲ Analyzing the Literature

Directions: Think about the section you just read. Read each question and state your response with textual evidence.

1. How is Maniac's journey different now from when he initially goes on the run at the beginning of the book?

_____

_____

_____

_____

2. In what ways are Russell and Piper like Maniac?

_____

_____

_____

_____

3. How does Maniac feel about the living conditions at the McNab's?

_____

_____

_____

_____

4. Maniac regrets embarrassing Mars Bar in the race. Why?

_____

_____

_____

_____

Name _____

Date _____

Reader Response

Directions: Choose one of the following prompts about this section to answer. Be sure you include a topic sentence in your response, use textual evidence to support your opinion, and provide a strong conclusion that summarizes your opinion.

Writing Prompts

- **Narrative Piece**—Discuss the problems that you think Maniac will face now that he has beaten and humiliated Mars Bar in a race. What advice would you give Maniac on how he should proceed to keep racial and personal tensions in check?
- **Opinion/Argument Piece**—Which character do you think is "badder"— Mars Bar Thompson or Maniac Magee? Include examples from the text that support your choice.

_____

_____

_____

_____

_____

_____

_____

_____

_____

_____

_____

_____

_____

Close Reading the Literature

Directions: Closely reread chapter 36 from the beginning of the chapter to the sentences that begin, "The door opened. *Finsterwald's door opened.*" Read each question and then revisit the text to find evidence that supports your answer.

1. What story evidence helps you understand that Maniac resorts to fibbing when he talks to Russell and Piper about Mexico?

   _____

   _____

   _____

2. Use examples from the text to show that the crowd of boys is fearful as Maniac walks up the stairs to the Finsterwald's house.

   _____

   _____

   _____

3. Give evidence from the text to explain why Russell and Piper McNab really stay in school.

   _____

   _____

4. What text evidence helps the reader understand how *importance* makes Russell and Piper feel?

   _____

   _____

Name _____

Date _____

Making Connections—Writing a Soliloquy!

In a play, a character will sometimes speak his thoughts and relate his feelings aloud when he is alone on the stage. This is called a *soliloquy*. Famous soliloquies can be found in several of Shakespeare's plays, including *Hamlet* and *Romeo and Juliet*.

Directions: Reread chapter 33 to refresh your memory about the various places and monuments that Maniac encounters as he travels. Put yourself in Maniac's place as he runs throughout the month of January, and write a soliloquy as he faces landmarks that are painful reminders of the past.

For example, whenever Maniac crosses the bridge over the Schuylkill, he avoids looking at the nearby P & W trestle since that is where his parents were killed. If Maniac were to write a soliloquy about this bridge, he might write the following: "To look or not to look. No, don't. Mom, Dad, I can only imagine the terror you felt as the trolley plunged into the water. I can't bear to think about it. Please don't die. I miss you so much. Now all I do is run, run, and run some more."

_____

_____

_____

_____

_____

_____

_____

_____

_____

Name _____

Date _____

Creating with the Story Elements

Directions: Thinking about the story elements of character, setting, and plot in a novel is very important to understanding what is happening and why. Complete **one** of the following activities based on what you've read so far. Be creative and have fun!

Characters

Make a collage that shows Maniac's true character. First, make a list of his characteristics, both good and bad. Then, find pictures, words and phrases, or objects to represent each characteristic. Arrange and glue everything to a large sheet of paper or cardboard.

Setting

Create a poster highlighting the safety hazards in the McNab household. Explain how each hazard poses a health risk. For example, cockroaches cover the rugless floor. These insects leave behind waste material and spread germs wherever they go. Not only is the situation unsightly, but it is also unsanitary.

Plot

Without reading ahead, write the next chapter of this book describing how you think Maniac will resolve the problems and tensions between the McNab family and the East Enders. What adventure will Maniac create next? Try to write in the same voice and style as author Jerry Spinelli.

Vocabulary Overview

Ten key words from this section are provided below with definitions and sentences about how the words are used in the book. Choose one of the vocabulary activity sheets (pages 55 or 56) for students to complete as they read this section. Monitor students as they work to ensure the definitions they have found are accurate and relate to the text. Finally, discuss these important vocabulary words with students. If you think these words or other words in the section warrant more time devoted to them, there are suggestions in the introduction for other vocabulary activities (page 5).

Word	Definition	Sentence about Text
fortified (ch. 40)	strengthened; refreshed	After he is **fortified** by his good time at the Pickwell's, Maniac returns to the McNab household.
extort (ch. 40)	to get something from someone using force or power	Maniac uses pizza to **extort** Russell and Piper into staying in school a day or two longer.
goaded (ch. 40)	stimulated or motivated someone into action	Maniac **goads** Russell and Piper toward attending school any way that he can.
swaggered (ch. 41)	walked in a confident way; strutted	Mars Bar Thompson **swaggers** his way into the birthday party at the McNab's house.
notions (ch. 41)	ideas or beliefs	Maniac thinks about the McNabs' wrong-headed **notions** about black people.
gauntlet (ch. 42)	a line of people; an intimidating crowd	As Mars Bar walks down the **gauntlet** of Cobras, Maniac tries to protect him.
illusion (ch. 43)	a false idea or belief	It is probably an **illusion** that causes Mrs. Pickwell's whistle to travel so far.
dovetailed (ch. 44)	joined together; converged	When Maniac and Mars Bar run and **dovetail** for a second time, they remain that way with no words.
diverged (ch. 44)	went in a different direction from one another	The boys **diverge** when the working people begin leaving their houses.
amplified (ch. 45)	an increased sound	An **amplified** gulp emerges from the emu.

Name _____

Date _____

Understanding Vocabulary Words

Directions: The following words appear in this section of the book. Use context clues and reference materials to determine an accurate definition for each word.

Word	Definition
fortified (ch. 40)	
extort (ch. 40)	
goaded (ch. 40)	
swaggered (ch. 41)	
notions (ch. 41)	
gauntlet (ch. 42)	
illusion (ch. 43)	
dovetailed (ch. 44)	
diverged (ch. 44)	
amplified (ch. 45)	

Name _____

Date _____

During-Reading Vocabulary Activity

Directions: As you read these chapters, choose five important words from the story. Then, use those five words to complete this word flow chart. On each arrow, write a vocabulary word. In the boxes between the words, explain how the words connect. An example for the words *swaggers* and *gauntlet* has been done for you.

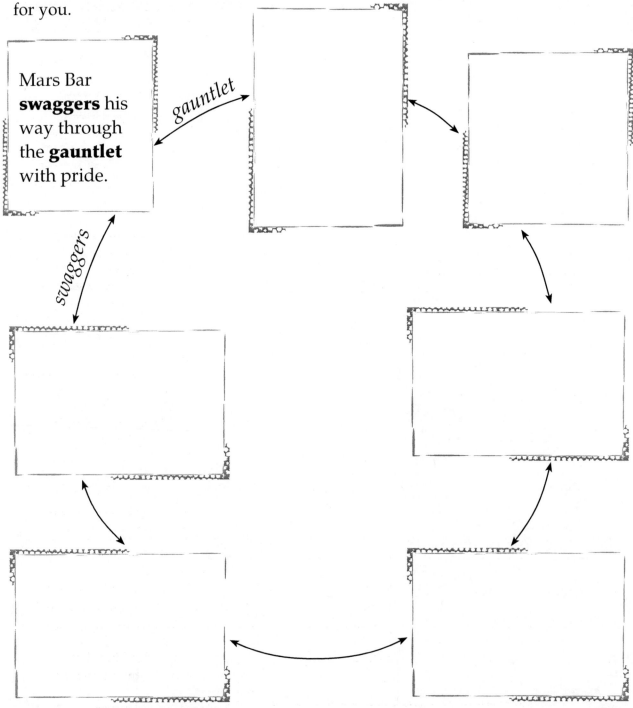

Mars Bar **swaggers** his way through the **gauntlet** with pride.

Analyzing the Literature

Provided below are discussion questions you can use in small groups, with the whole class, or for written assignments. Each question is given at two levels so you can choose the right question for each group of students. Activity sheets with these questions are provided (pages 58–59) if you want students to write their responses. For each question, a few key discussion points are provided for your reference.

Story Element	■ Level 1	▲ Level 2	Key Discussion Points
Plot	How does Maniac keep Russell and Piper in school?	Why does Maniac feel that he cannot leave the McNabs?	Maniac uses pizza to extort the boys into staying in school. He also reads to them, organizes a marbles tournament, and takes them to the library. Maniac cannot leave because ". . . to abandon the boys would be to abandon something in himself." Deep down, Maniac feels the boys are identical to Hester and Lester Beale.
Character	Explain how Mars Bar is "bad."	Why does Maniac consider himself "badder" than Mars Bar?	Mars Bar is confident and walks with a swagger. A rip-stone, evil scowl crosses his face, and he has an in-your-face nastiness. Maniac matches Mars Bar's glares, telling him he's not so bad since he has not crossed Hector Street and stays where it is safe.
Setting	What is the atmosphere like in the Pickwell's house when Maniac brings Mars Bar for dinner?	Why does Maniac bring Mars Bar to the Pickwell's before going to the birthday party?	The little Pickwell children make a fuss over both Mars Bar and Maniac. Mrs. Pickwell graciously and warmly accepts her new guest. Maniac wants Mars Bar to ". . . see the best the West End had to offer." Maniac knows that their reception at the McNab's may not be the same as it is at the Pickwells'.
Character	Describe the reaction upon Mars Bar's arrival at Piper's birthday party.	What is Maniac's reasoning for bringing Mars Bar to Piper's birthday party?	Mars's arrival stops the party. George McNab calls Mars "It." One of the Cobras crashes directly behind Mars, scaring him. Mars is furious with Maniac for bringing him there. Maniac questions his own feelings, thinking that maybe he is looking for a miracle to happen.

Name _____

Date _____

Analyzing the Literature

Directions: Think about the section you just read. Read each question and state your response with textual evidence.

1. How does Maniac keep Russell and Piper in school?

   _____

   _____

   _____

   _____

2. Explain how Mars Bar is "bad."

   _____

   _____

   _____

   _____

3. What is the atmosphere like in the Pickwell's house when Maniac brings Mars Bar for dinner?

   _____

   _____

   _____

   _____

4. Describe the reaction upon Mars Bar's arrival at Piper's birthday party.

   _____

   _____

   _____

   _____

Name _____

Date _____

▲ Analyzing the Literature

Directions: Think about the section you just read. Read each question and state your response with textual evidence.

1. Why does Maniac feel that he cannot leave the McNabs?

   _____

   _____

   _____

   _____

2. Why does Maniac consider himself "badder" than Mars Bar?

   _____

   _____

   _____

   _____

3. Why does Maniac bring Mars Bar to the Pickwell's before going to the birthday party?

   _____

   _____

   _____

   _____

4. What is Maniac's reasoning for bringing Mars Bar to Piper's birthday party?

   _____

   _____

   _____

   _____

Name _____

Date _____

Reader Response

Directions: Choose one of the following prompts about this section to answer. Be sure you include a topic sentence in your response, use textual evidence to support your opinion, and provide a strong conclusion that summarizes your opinion.

Writing Prompts

- **Informative/Explanatory Piece**—Maniac is different from his peers in many ways, especially in his views of people who have different skin colors. In what ways do you feel different from your peers?
- **Narrative Piece**—Amanda Beale convinces Maniac to come live with her family. Discuss the positive changes you foresee for Maniac as he assumes his new role as a permanent member of a happy, loving family.

_____

_____

_____

_____

_____

_____

_____

_____

_____

_____

_____

_____

_____

_____

Name _____

Date _____

Close Reading the Literature

Directions: Closely reread chapter 44 beginning with the sentence, "They were cruising Main Street one morning . . . ." Continue reading through the end of the chapter. Read each question and then revisit the text to find evidence that supports your answer.

1. How can you tell that Piper McNab is in trouble and needs help? Cite text evidence to support your response.

   _____

   _____

   _____

2. Explain the Bombs Away game that Russell and Piper play. Use the text to help support your response.

   _____

   _____

   _____

3. Using examples from the text, describe the dangers Russell faces as he is stuck on the trestle.

   _____

   _____

4. Cite the text to describe Maniac's response to Piper's pleas to save his brother Russell.

   _____

   _____

   _____

Name _____

Date _____

Making Connections—Similarities Bar Graph

Directions: In the last section of the book, Maniac keeps thinking about how the Beale and the Pickwell families are alike: Both families are friendly, giving, and accepting. He is also sure that deep inside, Russell and Piper McNab are identical to Hester and Lester Beale.

Use the questions listed below to find out how alike your family and your fellow students' families are. Then, use the data gathered to make a class bar graph. You may want to work in a small group to create the bar graph. Afterwards, write a summary statement about the data gathered on a separate sheet of paper.

Question	Yes	No
Does your family eat at least one meal a day together?		
Are you assigned specific chores at home?		
Are there serious consequences for bad behavior?		
Does your family make a big deal out of special occasions such as birthdays or holidays?		
Is name-calling tolerated in your house?		
Are you expected to do your best in school at all times?		
Are family members very supportive of one another every day?		
Do you do things together as a family, such as go to the movies, have game night, or attend church?		

Name _____

Date _____

Creating with the Story Elements

Directions: Thinking about the story elements of character, setting, and plot in a novel is very important to understanding what is happening and why. Complete **one** of the following activities based on what you've read so far. Be creative and have fun!

Characters

Think about how Mars Bar reacts as he enters Piper McNab's birthday party with Maniac. Draw a cartoon of Mars Bar's facial expression at that moment and use a speech bubble to show what he is thinking. Draw another cartoon of Mars Bar, this time showing his facial expression as he plots how he is going to get even with Maniac. Write the words that he is saying to himself in the speech bubble that you draw.

Setting

Recall the chaotic atmosphere of the McNab house. Write a list of rules that you would institute if you were named the new head of their household. Next to each rule, write a consequence for breaking that rule.

Plot

Both Mars Bar and Amanda Beale invite Maniac to live with their respective families, but in the end, Maniac accepts Amanda's invitation. Write a short skit in which Mars Bar and Amanda argue their cases, both explaining why Maniac would be better off living in either of their homes. With a partner, perform your skit for the entire class.

Name _____

Date _____

Post-Reading Theme Thoughts

Directions: Read each of the statements in the first column. Choose a main character from *Maniac Magee*. Think about that character's point of view. From that character's perspective, decide if the character would agree or disagree with the statements. Record the character's opinion by marking an *X* in Agree or Disagree for each statement. Explain your choices in the fourth column using text evidence.

Character I Chose: _____

Statement	Agree	Disagree	Explain Your Answer
Married couples should never divorce.			
If you witness someone being bullied, ignore the situation.			
Racial prejudice is a problem that exists only among adults in our society.			
Instead of facing a difficult situation head on, it is best to run from it.			

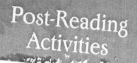
Post-Reading
Activities

Culminating Activity: Dispelling Assumptions

Directions: Throughout the book, various characters reveal the assumptions they have about black people or about white people. Fill in the chart below with information cited from the text. Begin by filling in the middle column with the event and assumption that each character has. In the third column, explain Maniac's words or actions in response to the event. For example, during a street festival in the East End, an old man tells Maniac to go home to "his own kind." The man assumes that Maniac does not belong there, but Maniac explains to the old man that he already *is* home.

Character	Event/Assumption	Maniac's Actions
Amanda Beale		
Mars Bar		
Grayson		
Russell and Piper McNab		

Name _____

Date _____

Culminating Activity:
Dispelling Assumptions *(cont.)*

Directions: After you have completed the chart of events and assumptions on the previous page, choose one of the following projects to complete. Use information from the chart as directed.

Choose one of the events from the chart. Pretend that you are an advice columnist. Using a specific character's point of view, write a letter describing how the events unfolded. End the letter with a question about what you should do or how you should have handled things differently. Next write a response using an advice columnist's voice explaining how to successfully defuse or resolve the situation.

Read through the chart of events and assumptions. Develop a list of guidelines that will help dispel assumptions and misperceptions that people may have of one another. For example, "Stop stereotyping—it may lead to wrong conclusions." Create a banner, complete with appropriate illustrations, for each guideline. Display the completed banners around the classroom.

Use one event from the chart to write a reader's theater script for that event. Add a second, alternate ending. Enlist other members of your class to read it aloud. Pause before informing the audience that you have an alternate ending to share. After reading it, ask class members to vote on which ending they think is preferable and discuss why.

Comprehension Assessment

Directions: Circle the best response to each question.

1. What does Jeffrey Lionel Magee do to earn the nickname Maniac?

   A. runs from Hollidaysburg to Two Mills

   B. screams at his school's musical performance

   C. a number of crazy stunts

   D. he does not attend school

2. Which detail from the book best supports your answer to question 1?

   E. "As for the first person to actually stop and talk with Maniac, that would be Amanda Beale."

   F. "He bunted the frog, laid down a perfect bunt in front of the plate . . . ."

   G. "The town was buzzing about the new kid in town."

   H. "When he wasn't reading, he was wandering."

3. What is the main idea of this text?

   "Whites never go inside blacks' homes. Much less inside their thoughts and feelings. And blacks are just as ignorant of whites. What white kid could hate blacks after spending five minutes in the Beales' house? And what black kid could hate whites after answering Mrs. Pickwell's dinner whistle?"

   _____

   _____

   _____

   _____

4. Choose **two** details from below to support your answer to question 3.

   A. East Enders stay in the East; West Enders stay in the West.

   B. The less East Enders and West Enders know about one another, the more they invent.

   C. Mars goads Maniac to fight him.

   D. The McNab boys do not expect Maniac to come walking through the door with some black kid.

Comprehension Assessment (cont.)

5. Which statement best expresses a theme of the book?

    E. Growing up is a great time of life.

    F. Enjoy life while you can.

    G. Running from your troubles is a good thing to do.

    H. Prejudice leads to wrong conclusions about people.

6. What detail from the book provides the best evidence for your answer to number 5?

    A. "She stomped her foot. 'You *gotta* stay!'"

    B. "They cruised around town, talking and eating Krimpets. 'So, said the old man, now what're you gonna do?'"

    C. "It was during Maniac's dessert that Grayson abruptly said, 'Them black people, do they eat mashed potatoes too?'"

    D. "As the old man left for his room at the Y, he would grouse, 'You oughta go to school.'"

7. What is the purpose of these sentences from the book: "Maniac loved almost everything about his new life. But everything did not love him back."

    _____

    _____

    _____

    _____

8. Which other quotation from the story serves a similar purpose?

    E. "And then Amanda was pedaling frantically up to him, slapping on a quick smile and gasping, 'Hey, I'm going to the store. Wanna come along?'"

    F. "Maniac gave his answer: 'I *am* home.'"

    G. "Hester and Lester came running up Sycamore. 'Maniac! C'mon! We're gonna run too!'"

    H. "'You move on now, Whitey,' the man said. 'You pick up your gear and move on out.'"

Response to Literature: The Issue of Prejudice

One important theme throughout the book *Maniac Magee* is that prejudice leads to wrong conclusions, false perceptions, and even hatred. It is through Maniac's eyes that the reader learns how an arbitrary dividing line, the Hector Street barrier, leads to suspicions and erroneous conclusions about other people. Although Maniac sees no color difference, there are plenty of others who focus solely on that one, physical characteristic. As he moves between the two worlds, Maniac tries to show by example that no one has anything to fear from the other side.

Unfortunately, prejudice in your school and community may be evident even today. Think about examples of prejudice that you may have witnessed or read about. How are they similar to events in the story? What are some causes of this prejudice? How can relations among the differing groups be improved?

Directions: Complete research on the topic of prejudice. Find out some of its causes and what people can do to overcome their own fears and assumptions. After you have gathered enough information, identify three examples of prejudice in *Maniac Magee* and describe in an essay how you would address each one so that you could improve the situation. Use the evidence that you have found during your research to support your views.

Your response should include the following guidelines:

- State a clear opinion.
- Be at least 750 words.
- Cite at least three different events in the story to support your opinion.
- Cite research to support your viewpoint.
- Provide a conclusion that summarizes your beliefs.

Name _____

Date _____

Response to Literature Rubric

Directions: Use this rubric to evaluate student responses.

	Exceptional Writing	**Quality Writing**	**Developing Writing**
Focus and Organization	☐ States a clear opinion and elaborates well. Engages the reader from the opening hook through the middle to the conclusion. Demonstrates clear understanding of the intended audience and purpose of the piece.	☐ Provides a clear and consistent opinion. Maintains a clear perspective and supports it through elaborating details. Makes the opinion clear in the opening hook and summarizes well in the conclusion.	☐ Provides an inconsistent point of view. Does not support the topic adequately or misses pertinent information. Provides lack of clarity in the beginning, middle, and conclusion.
Text Evidence	☐ Provides comprehensive and accurate support. Includes relevant and worthwhile text references.	☐ Provides limited support. Provides few supporting text references.	☐ Provides very limited support for the text. Provides no supporting text references.
Written Expression	☐ Uses descriptive and precise language with clarity and intention. Maintains a consistent voice and uses an appropriate tone that supports meaning. Uses multiple sentence types and transitions well between ideas.	☐ Uses a broad vocabulary. Maintains a consistent voice and supports a tone and feelings through language. Varies sentence length and word choices.	☐ Uses a limited and unvaried vocabulary. Provides an inconsistent or weak voice and tone. Provides little to no variation in sentence type and length.
Language Conventions	☐ Capitalizes, punctuates, and spells accurately. Demonstrates complete thoughts within sentences, with accurate subject-verb agreement. Uses paragraphs appropriately and with clear purpose.	☐ Capitalizes, punctuates, and spells accurately. Demonstrates complete thoughts within sentences and appropriate grammar. Paragraphs are properly divided and supported.	☐ Incorrectly capitalizes, punctuates, and spells. Uses fragmented or run-on sentences. Utilizes poor grammar overall. Paragraphs are poorly divided and developed.

The responses provided here are just examples of what the students may answer. Many accurate responses are possible for the questions throughout this unit.

During-Reading Vocabulary Activity—Section 1: Chapters 1–9 (page 16)

1. Jeffrey does crazy things which cause people to nickname him **Maniac**. He intercepts Brian Denehy's pass one-handed, he rescues Arnold Jones from the Finsterwald's backyard, and he circles the bases on a bunted frog.

2. The backyard is **infamous** because it is a graveyard of tennis balls, baseballs, footballs, and Frisbees. Anyone left in the backyard can be overcome with the "finsterwallies."

Close Reading the Literature—Section 1: Chapters 1–9 (page 21)

1. Jeffrey gasps when Amanda opens the suitcase full of books. He falls to his knees to look through the suitcase.

2. Jeffrey doesn't know where he lives or why he is in the all-black East End. He is poorly dressed and grungy. He offers to carry Amanda's suitcase.

3. Amanda keeps her books in a suitcase because her brother and sister crayon every piece of paper they can find. Also because the dog, Bow Wow, likes to chew everything.

4. Maniac thinks Amanda is "different" because she is carrying a suitcase. This is what catches Maniac's eye.

During-Reading Vocabulary Activity—Section 2: Chapters 10–21 (page 26)

1. Mars Bar and his group are **scowling** because Mars Bar is angry with Maniac from their earlier encounter.

2. Everyone **converges** for the block party, which is a day and night of games, music, grilled chicken and ribs, and dancing.

Close Reading the Literature—Section 2: Chapters 10–21 (page 31)

1. Maniac loves the noise of the church, the Fourth of July block party, the colors of the East End, and the warm brown of Mrs. Beale's thumb. He loves going to the vacant lot and playing the summer days away with stickball, basketball, and football.

2. When Mrs. Beale asks, "You that Maniac?" he answers, "I'm Jeffrey. You know that." Maniac was afraid of losing his name, the only thing he had left from his parents.

3. Maniac catches Hands Down's passes all day long and scores 49 touchdowns.

4. Church makes Maniac want to do more than run. One day he jumps up onto the pew bench and shouts, "Hallelujah! Amen!"

Close Reading the Literature—Section 3: Chapters 22–32 (page 41)

1. At first, Maniac is silent, but then he explains that he's not going to school, not unless they find him. If Grayson tries to make him go, Maniac says he will just start running.

2. Grayson takes Maniac to the YMCA to wash up, and he buys butterscotch krimpets and clothing for Maniac.

3. A school is sort of like a big, day home because then it empties out. You can't stay there at night because it's not really a home.

4. Grayson looks at Maniac with recognition ". . . as though the fish he had landed might be the same one he had thrown away long before."

During-Reading Vocabulary Activity—Section 4: Chapters 33–39 (page 46)

1. It is the most **perilous** challenge of all because Maniac's enemy, Mars Bar Thompson, and his gang live there. They might do harm to Maniac. West Enders are afraid of the blacks and are unsure of what they might do.

2. The **pandemonium** includes the crowd going crazy, wild, and totally bananas. Mars Bar complains that he had not been ready for the race.

Close Reading the Literature—Section 4: Chapters 33–39 (page 51)

1. Maniac crosses his fingers while telling Russell and Piper they will have to wait because it is volcano season in Mexico and the whole place is a sheet of red-hot lava.

2. The crowd of boys huddle, trembling. As Maniac knocks on the door, "fifteen hearts beat in time to that silent knocking."

3. Other kids pelt Russell and Piper with questions about Maniac, and they like the attention they get for having Maniac in their home.

4. Importance pumps up the two boys. It gives them bounce like a basketball, and they want more.

Close Reading the Literature—Section 5: Chapters 40–46 (page 61)

1. Piper comes screaming down the middle of the street. He is crying, wild-eyed, and soaking wet.

2. Piper sails the raft down the river while Russell waits on the trestle spanning the river. When Piper passes underneath, Russell drops rocks onto the raft.

3. Russell is on the middle of the trestle, frozen in terror. He does not have a railing to cling to, and he does not respond to Piper's cries or the toot of the oncoming P & W Trolley.

4. Maniac's unblinking eyes do not register what is on the trestle, nor does he seem to hear Piper pleading. Maniac turns, and without a word, leaves the platform and goes downstairs. He crosses Main and slowly walks up Swede.

Comprehension Assessment (pages 67–68)

1. C. a number of crazy stunts

2. F. "He bunted the frog, laid down a perfect bunt in front of the plate . . . ."

3. Main Idea: The white and black people of East End and West End are ignorant of one another's thoughts and feelings.

4. Supporting Details: A. East Enders stayed in the East; West Enders stayed in the West. B. The less East Enders and West Enders know about one another, the more they invent.

5. H. Prejudice leads to wrong conclusions about people.

6. C. "It was during Maniac's dessert that Grayson abruptly said, 'Them black people, do they eat mashed potatoes too?'"

7. Maniac loves his new home with the Beale family and they love him. However, not everyone in the community likes the idea of a white boy living with a black family.

8. H. "'You move on now, Whitey,' the man said. 'You pick up your gear and move on out.'"